D0048126

PIVOT

CHANGE ISN'T COMING, IT'S HERE

GOLDEN BRICK ROAD
PUBLISHING HOUSE

"*PIVOT* is THE guidebook for navigating change powerfully. Turning unwelcome changes into opportunities for growth and contribution."

-Paige Elenson, founder Africa Yoga Project
@africayogaproject

"*PIVOT* will give you the insight and actions needed to face change head on. The practices of PIVOT will work for you personally, they will work for you in the groups you are in and they will work for you in leadership of your business. Pauline invites you to have a new perspective on change and gives you weekly tasks to shift that perspective starting with the source of your purpose. Developing new perspectives and habits that are lasting with the freedom to revisit when change happens again!"

-Kinndli McCollum, co-founder Power Yoga Canada
@poweryogacanada

"By incorporating the five strategies for managing change, *PIVOT* has provided me with tools to embrace and successfully navigate challenges in my professional world and personal life. I learned that you can remain true to your purpose. When change comes, I have learned the methods to embrace opportunity in a unique way. All I need to do is pivot!"

-Shirley Smith, President of Buckland Group of Companies
@bucklandinsta

"Whether you are looking to *PIVOT* your perspective on a relationship, an obstacle or the culture of the team you lead, this book will give you a refreshing point of view and concrete actionables to make a lasting shift."

-Nicole Lewis, photographer @blondecoffeebean

"Pauline took me on the in-depth journey of understanding change in my personal and professional life. The book allows for hands on work and is very intuitive to the reader. The actual work allows for growth over their edge, and for me, to trust their intuition."

-Kristina Pancevski, project manager & owner of
Power Yoga Canada Guelph @pycguelph

"If you are looking to *PIVOT* in your career, your health or any other area, I highly recommend this book! I love how real, vulnerable and insightful this book is and how many practical takeaways as exercises are offered—amazing!"

-Monica Gibbs, motivational speaker and wellness coach
contact@monicagibbs.com

Five practices to strategize and support you through change.

PIVOT

CHANGE ISN'T COMING, IT'S HERE

Pauline Caballero

Published in Canada for Global Distribution by Golden Brick Road Publishing House Inc. Printed in North America.

ISBN: 9781988736969

Author: paulinecaballero@me.com

Media: hello@gbrph.ca

Book orders: orders@gbrph.ca

Contents

Week Four: Obstacles

Week Five: Tactics

Introduction

Here I was again. Sobbing profusely wondering how I had gotten here yet again. Laying on the cold tiles of the bathroom floor was somewhere I was finding myself every couple of years. It was about that time, I should have known, I told myself. Just as I had become comfortable and settled into life. There it was, the other shoe fell and things were nowhere near as perfect as they had seemed the day before. When I finally pulled myself up off that floor, I swore that was going to be the last time I found myself in that state. I was no longer going to be shocked and surprised by the turn of events or changes in life. I was done being a victim. It was time for a change and this time it was me that was going to force it. It was that day that the concept for this book was born, but that wasn't the last time on the bathroom floor. Nor did I complete the book until a decade later, but looking back, that was the day that sparked and shifted everything, whether I liked it or not. Change was happening and I had very little control over it, if any at all. All I had to do was open up my eyes and go along for the ride. Like many of us, I had the idea that everything in my life had to be predictable and consistent in order to achieve success. At some point in your life I am sure you have felt the burden of change being forced upon you or the burden of wanting something different. The truth is no matter who you are we have all stood at the fork in the road and wondered which direction now?

The illustrious fork in the road, which path to the city of OZ, which pill to take in the matrix. If I choose the wrong path my life will surely be over. What if that wasn't the case? What if no matter which path you take you can't go wrong? What if any change you would find along your path would all be for good? It wasn't until recently that I have seen what is possible if and when I am able to embrace change. I was caught in the feeling of things moving forward with or without me. Realizing that my boys were growing up, becoming more independent, and I was stuck doing and acting the same. When nothing was the same. They no longer need me to fold their laundry and cut their apples. Embracing changes is, in fact, the only thing that has allowed me to move forward in life. This book is not another self-help book nor is it the framework to start up a new business. The conversation that I am looking to bring to life with this book is to demonstrate how all of us can be powerful in our movement, the movements we will refer to here as pivots. In the change from one direction to the other, we are given an opportunity to choose how we want to react, engage, or disengage. Sometimes that pivot happens multiple times in a day, sometimes the pivot is much more monumental and shifts your life's entire trajectory. In either case it wasn't until I accepted the pivot as a powerful tool to be, move, and fuel myself in a way that will not only empower me but the community, organization, and teams around me as well. After all, isn't that the point of our existence? To elevate ourselves and bring everyone else with us? Everything I speak about here, I learned through various teachers and friends: Bonnie Vozar, Kari Granger, Fernando Flores, The Landmark Forum, Power Yoga Canada, and Kinndli McCollum. The discovery, or as Mr. Flores would say, the appropriation of it all I learned from my husband, Gerard. Nothing here will be new, or some unbelievable framework. The only thing that is new is that I have never delivered my interpretation of the pivot and you have never read it before. So in this case, we are new students on a journey of learning together, one breath at a time.

Let's begin to dive deeper into the framework, and remember, you are free to choose, but you are not free from the consequences of your choice.

WHAT IS THE CONCEPT OF PIVOT?

I woke up one day in the Spring of 2017 with a heaviness that I couldn't put my finger on. I rolled out of bed walking past my sleeping husband, whom I barely spoke to on the best of days and caught my image in the mirror. I stared at myself and saw what I knew was me but there was nothing about that woman that I recognized. I was in motion and doing things that made no difference to the world and were not aligned with my core values and who I wanted to be. I was a walking zombie living on a treadmill going nowhere. It was that moment that I realized I, the woman I knew was gone and everything I thought I knew for sure was crumbling around me. It was as though I had been living in a bad dream and had woken up. My entire life was unrecognizable. My marriage, my kids, my work, the company that I had built. None of it was anything I had known the night before. At that point my marriage was rocky at best. I had chosen work over my family, I could pretend to say I was doing everything for the good of my family, but I was not. I was simply focused on one thing and one thing only, power. I saw power as a way to define myself and to claim my place in the world. At this point my boys were five and twelve. My on-again-and-off-again marriage had been surviving for thirteen years and the business that I had built with my business partner was chugging along thanks to her efforts. So to the outsider, everything was fine. We hear people say they are fine all the time. A four letter word for the average person that means just that, I am fine, I am ok. Well, for me, "fine" is code for "something is wrong." Anytime that any one of my employees begins with "Everything is fine," my response is, "What's wrong? And what is happening or not happening that is having you say, fine?". Things being fine is an alarm to me that they are indeed not. This is exactly how I was living my life, that everything was fine and that is exactly why my subconscious pulled the mental alarm and woke me up in such a jarring way that morning. I still didn't know what it was that triggered me waking up in that state, but the message was crystal clear: it was time to wake up and move, and even with that internal alarm ringing I froze and left everything in my life status quo. That is until I didn't.

My husband on the other hand began his career as a plumber at the age of twenty, simply following the footsteps of his dad. At the time of writing this, he had been with his current employer for over twenty-three years. That is more than half his adult life. He is a rare breed in our modern day era that started something and stuck with it. More importantly, he was blessed to have been able to do so. In the age where going to Blockbusters to rent a VHS tape is a historical notion, and calling a taxi on a rotary phone is no longer possible, staying with one job for over twenty years is basically unheard of anymore. Not only because of desire, but primarily because of innovation: people are being forced out of their comfortable jobs, whether they like it or not, and regardless of whether they want to or not. My husband is an example of someone who has not pivoted, at least in the realm of work. His eternal subconscious alarm hasn't rung where he is left questioning everything, and if you were to ask him if the picture painted above provides him satisfaction or if he experiences contentment, or dare I say it—happiness? . . . I am not sure how he would respond. He might just say, "Everything is fine." For me, that response would be a wake up call. For him, that is not the case; that is until it is.

THE PRACTICES OF PIVOT

Challenging the status quo and disrupting the flow of fine is the practice that we will go through in this book. We will take the time each week to review three specific practices. You can move as fast or as slow as you want. This is not a one time activity, but rather a lifelong practice; a series of tools that you can use forever. Sometimes you may have to pull out your journal and complete the practices as designed and follow the instructions. Other times you may simply need one practice and whisper the answers to yourself, without ever having the need to pull out a pencil or jot a note on your phone. As we continue on this journey you will begin to realize that change is forever happening and always occuring. Change is not a one-time occurrence, but rather something that is shifting over and over again.

I invite you to carve our five weeks to read this book. Allow the practices and words to wash over you. Give time for ideas to percolate and brew inside of you. Over the next five weeks we will dive into practices to provoke curiosity and be intentional about what you are doing and where you are doing it, whether it is at home, at play, or at work. We will look at what needs to shift and where you need to pivot. This is not about creating the perfect balance for all areas of your life to act in synchronicity and harmony. In fact, we will play with the concept of there is no such thing as balance. We will consider it as a myth that someone stated out loud, and like good sheep, we act as though we should attempt to achieve the seemingly impossible goal of balance. How does one measure balance? What is the perfect balance in life? Does it differ from person to person? Well, considering that complete balance is not possible, why would we continue to spend the rest of our lives attempting to find that idealized state?

The practice of *PIVOT* is about understanding what it means to shift gears purposefully, and pivot to live a life that is prosperous inside you and outside in the real world. Understanding how to handle the fundamentals so that you can make choices that align with your heart, deep desires, and purpose. I will share how I have pivoted in my life over and over again, and will continue to do so, until I don't. You will be guided through each of the five weeks in this program to support you through the journey of shifting and moving into new directions with ease. The practices shared in this book can be used repeatedly. The intention is that you revisit these practices frequently, and in any order and at any time. Our lives are a continuous practice. There is no one challenge to overcome, no single game to win. In fact, it is the complete opposite. There are a million competing priorities all happening at the same time over and over again. The challenge that remains is how to navigate through, maintain your focus, and shift to prosper and thrive from the ride. How do you know when it is time to pivot? How do you know if it is time to focus and stay put? If you are interested in learning practical tools that will support you in the ebbs and flows and unpredictability of life then I encourage you to keep reading.

* * *

The actions of *PIVOT* can apply anywhere in your life, including in your business. Change is always with us. In my lifetime we went from referencing a phone book to find the pizza delivery store's number, to Googling the number on the internet, to completing the order on my cell phone via an app and having the pizza show up at my door without speaking to a single person. In my teens I spent hours walking through Blockbusters to determine what movie we would watch that weekend; today my children crawl into bed and scroll through Netflix and Disney plus, and in a matter of moments, have every movie they could imagine at their fingertips without getting out of bed. It is imminent that electric cars will overtake the traditional combustible car. What will we do with all our gas stations as we transition to electric cars? The disruption this will create will be felt across the globe from manufacturing to consumer. It is no longer a matter of "if" but rather a question of "when?". We don't have to look very far to find another example that we all are familiar with: the sheer act of photography and the almighty selfie. In the book, *Who Owns the Future,* a computer science pioneer Jason Lanier says, "At the height of its power, Kodak employed more than 140,000 people and was worth $28 billion. They even invented the first digital camera. But today Kodak is bankrupt, and the new face of digital photography has become Instagram. When Instagram was sold to Facebook for a billion dollars in 2012, it employed only 13 people."

Change isn't coming, it's here. Pivoting is no longer a choice, but rather a requirement for survival and the way to thrive is to choose it. Consciously choosing it over and over again.

Week One:
PERSPECTIVE

"'Come to the edge,' he said.
'We can't, we're afraid!' they responded.
'Come to the edge,' he said.
'We can't, we will fall!' they responded.
'Come to the edge,' he said.
And so they came.
And he pushed them.
And they flew."

-Guillaume Apollinaire

According to the dictionary, perspective, can be defined as: a particular attitude toward or way of regarding something; a point of view. Let's consider for this conversation that the "point of view" is you and your beliefs about everything and everyone. Consider for a moment that they are strict beliefs and could be limits placed in your periphery causing boundaries and constraints that we place on ourselves. Now, what is important to note is that boundaries and constraints are not bad things. In fact, they are necessary to achieve results in your life. An example of such would be an elite athlete who places constraints in their diet to ensure their body is operating in an optimal way. In this program we will look at "how do we go beyond our already existing knowledge?" and "how will we prepare ourselves to pivot and move into our next adventure and take the leap off the ledge that we have known so well?" But mostly we will get into our blindspots and what we don't see.

My first exposure to shifting came at a very young age, although as I look back through my adult lense it is clear that shift and change are constants. The one that sticks out for me the most was the shift from being a competitive athlete to not being one. At one point in time figure skating and being at the rink defined me. My entire life was coordinated around what happened on the ice and every single thing I did was to promote improvement on the ice. Everything. Right down to the food I ate and did not eat, the events I attended and did not attend, and the extracurricular activities I did and did not do. It was a very simple math equation. If I deemed it would improve my performance then I would be interested in it. If it added zero value then I would simply not be interested. Who knows if that was the right approach; back then it was the only one I knew. Focus on one thing and do it over and over again. The question is, did I simply fall into the discipline of skating or was it a passion, a clear path that I wanted to take? At the time I would not have been able to answer that question truthfully because I was simply too young to know what I wanted and what I did not want. I had little guidance through those years because my mother was suffering from mental illness and my father was busy working to pay for our life. But I was also not present to my core beliefs: the thoughts and beliefs that guide me in what I do and what I do not do.

WHAT DO YOU STAND FOR?

In the January 1945 issue of a journal called *Mental Hygiene*, the following paragraph described the importance of people finding a focus, a sense of purpose, and what we can refer to as a north star. At the time of publication, World War II was still being fought. The paragraph was written by a medical doctor Gordon A. Eadie, titled "The Overall Mental-Health Needs of the Industrial Plant, with Special Reference to War Veterans":

> *We are trying to show him not only what we are fighting against, but what we are fighting for. So many of these boys have only a very hazy idea of the real issues of the war. About all they see is "going back to the good old days." This is a dangerous state.* **If they don't stand for something, they will fall for anything.** *They need to realize that we are fighting two wars—the war of arms and the war of ideas—that other war of which the war of arms is one phase.*

Now I know that we are not dealing with a world war or a war of arms, but we are dealing with the world of change with the recent COVID-19 pandemic where everything as we know it changed and shifted. The economy and our freedom to be completely shut down and we were sent to our homes to hide and protect ourselves. Right in that moment we were given the opportunity to choose what it is that we stand for so that we can walk on a path that we believe in. Many people are claiming COVID-19 is something we have never seen before, but we have and wrote about it in 1945. We must learn to stand for what we believe in, the question is, what is that? This is where the first practice will have us look. What are the fundamental beliefs that you have? What is it that you stand for so that you don't fall for anything? Do you ever find yourself saying yes to everything? Do you have a fear of missing out, more commonly known as FOMO these days? The sheer act of trying to do it all comes at a cost. It doesn't allow for the perspective of aligning with actions that match with your core beliefs. The bigger question is, what are your core beliefs? What do you value and what is of the utmost importance to you? Let's first define what a core value is:

1. The regard that something is held to deserve; the importance; worth, or usefulness of something.

2. A person's principles or standards of behavior; one's judgement of what is important in life.

Some examples of core values include: integrity, boldness, honesty, trust, accountability, commitment to others, passion, fun. Core values are important not only to the individual, but also to corporations from the small to Fortune 500 companies. More and more we are seeing a trend towards individuals and organizations alike placing a stake in the ground and claiming: here is what we stand for, here is what we will be known for, and here is what our statement will be to the world. I co-founded a yoga studio in 2009 and within the first twelve months my business partner and I defined our core values and shared it with the teachers and students we had at the time. They were simple and taken from a book called *The Collaborative Way* by Llyod and Jason Fickett. It turned out to be the best decision we ever made. It provided us and our teams guidelines as we grew the foundation of how the entire organization operated. Power Yoga

Canada had a unique tool to onboard new teachers, greet every guest, and a way to act and be that was uniquely our own. The core values were; speaking straight, listening generously, honoring commitments, being for each other, acknowledgments and appreciation. All inside the container of operating with integrity and creative collaboration into greatness.

We didn't know it at the time, but that single act of creating the framework provided everyone who works with Power Yoga Canada the understanding of what we stood for. Ultimately giving them the freedom to be and act from our core values—over time, they became our collective values. Different from providing clear and drawn out work instructions by setting the framework from which a company stands, it provided everyone in the company with the freedom to do their job and operate in alignment with the core values. This practice is being identified as a distinguishing factor in the success of other businesses, not just our yoga studios. Larry Fink, CEO and Chairman of the Board for Blackrock Investment Firm, stated in a letter to their clients: "The importance of serving stakeholders and embracing purpose is becoming increasingly central to the way that companies understand their role in society. As I have written in past letters, a company cannot achieve long-term profits without embracing purpose and considering the needs of a broad range of stakeholders." Investment firms are coming out and blatantly stating that purpose results in profit. This practice can work for companies and you. Let's take a look at how you can begin connecting with your core values. One thing to remember is that nothing is fixed. If you have already identified your core values . . . great. Perhaps there has been a shift in your life and you are looking to re-evaluate and realign. It is important to be malleable and fluid with it all. Anything and everything can change, evolve, and shift.

SPEAKING STRAIGHT

LISTENING GENEROUSLY

HONOURING COMMITMENTS

BEING FOR EACH OTHER

ACKNOWLEDGEMENTS & APPRECIATION

poweryoga
CANADA

PRACTICE 1

What Do You Stand For?

You will need multiple sheets of blank paper for this practice. The intention of this practice is to complete a CORE VALUE MAP and have a list of words or phrases that are your core values. This list should serve as the barometer for all your decisions. Your actions and your non-actions. The things you do and the things you do not do. They will also serve as a way to identify your future intentions. We will walk you through the process step by step. This is a practice that you can do over and over again, and one that you can share with your family and teams.

Step 1: Draw a line horizontally through the center of a blank page. The top of the page will be considered positive, the line neutral, and the bottom of the page less than positive. Once drawn out put this sheet aside. This will become your Core Value Map.

Step 2: On a second blank sheet of paper, identify events in your life, career, and vocation that were milestone events. These were significant or life changing, and the type of thing someone would write in a biography about your life. These events may be positive, negative, or neutral. Aim to identify seven totem events.

Step 3: Once you have the list of events, plot them in the appropriate location on the Core Value Map. Your end result should look something like this:

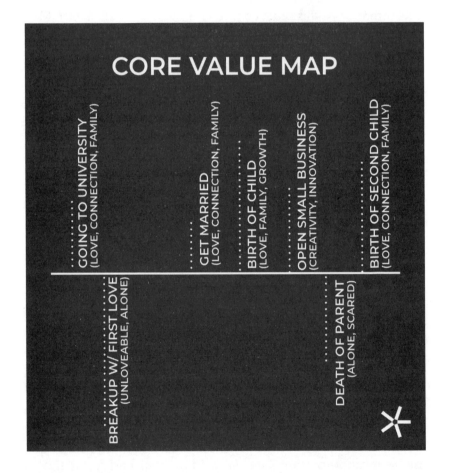

Step 4: For each milestone, put a mark above or below the horizontal line to indicate where in time that event occurred. Then label the event.

Step 5: For each milestone that you view as positive, put a plus (+) mark above the line representing how highly satisfied you were or how positive that event was for you.

Step 6: For each milestone that you view as negative, put a subtraction (-) mark below the line representing how unsatisfying or negative that event was for you.

Step 7: For each milestone above the line, identify what value was present that made it so satisfying for you, and for each milestone below the line, identify what value was missing that made it so unsatisfying. For example, during my divorce, the value of *love* was missing.

Step 8: Now look at the list of values you have identified and consider if there is anything even deeper. What values are essential to you that you are not seeing on your sheet of paper? If there are any, jot them down on the side of your sheet.

Step 9: Looking across all the events, choose your *top five values* that matter the most to you. You can base this on how much they showed up on the map, or how strongly you feel about them.

Step 10: On a fresh page write out your Five Core Values. Is there too many? Is there one that is missing? Try them out this week and test them out in the real world. These will be your guiding light so it is up to you to ensure that they fit.

As you look back on this practice ask yourself the following;

1. What choices have you made in your life where you used your core values as the guide to make the decision? Whether you had them defined or not. Can you see where you may have already used these values as a barometer to make a decision or choice?

2. What decisions have you made in life that went against your core values? So often we have a gut feeling that we know we should not do something and yet we still continue through. Can you see a time where the opposite occurred?

When my husband and I were first married we did what we thought was the right thing. The thing that every good couple does. We moved out to the country to buy a detached house and begin to live the traditional dream. Get married, buy a house, have a baby, we were embarking on the traditional life treadmill. We felt we were doing what we were supposed to do. The only problem was that these decisions were not in any way aligned with what we wanted. Our shared core value of *fun* was missing. We found ourselves having no fun in doing what we were supposed to do. We collectively agreed to move away from the downtown core, where we liked to be close to dinners and weekend gatherings, to live out in the country well over an hour away. We neglected to take into account the long commutes in and out for work, which accounted for over two hours of our day. Taking our son to my parents house before heading to the office added another forty-five minutes to that task. It started to wear us down. As young parents in our twenties we could not imagine life continuing on like this. By the time weekends rolled around we were exhausted, and unable or willing to move. We stopped all social activities due to lack of time. Exercise was a foreign concept. We had become prisoners to the commute and worse to our automobiles. Then one day in early spring my husband fell asleep in stop and go traffic and rammed into the car in front of him totalling it as he woke up from the crash. It took that incident for us to realize that we had made a grave mistake. In the long run it cost us more to shift our decision, but the bottom line was we needed to be aligned with our value of fun in order for us to live a life where we felt fulfilled and happy. We were asleep in our life going through the motions. Are you asleep? Are you blindly walking through life? We were blind to our core values and unable to see we were blind to them. Let's take another look: where is there an opportunity to identify with a place or action where you need to align with your core values? Where are you going along to get along? What is it costing you? What is it blocking you from? Is there a place in your business that you are cutting off creative flow because you are so focused on the process that you forget about your core values? Let's continue with the practices and see what becomes more evident.

PRACTICE 2

Confronting How You Show Up in the World

When COVID-19 hit our business core values became a guiding light. We had created them well over a decade ago, but in the face of the pandemic we needed them now more than ever. It was our chance to use our values in the face of difficult decisions. We had an opportunity to act one way or another. We closed our doors on a Sunday evening and by six on Monday morning we were live broadcasting for free on social media channels. Being for each other, one of our core values pointed to how we had to show up in the world. In the face of uncertainty and as everyone began to be quarantined in their homes, yoga, now more than ever, was important and critical. Once you have identified your core values and the way in which you are committed to showing up in the world, it is time to look at the opposite. How are you *actually* showing up in the world? How are people experiencing you and is it the way you want your legacy to be? In the corporate world this exercise is often referred to as a 360 review or feedback session. Anytime I would find myself in a situation where someone has an opinion or feedback I would immediately feel myself going inward, shutting down, and wanting to crawl into a cave. What is it that has us turning away from listening to others share their experience of us? Listening to how other people experience me and my actions is a practice I am getting more and more comfortable with. Within my corporate role of being a Chief Revenue Officer, I encourage and invite my staff to provide me with feedback to let me know how I am showing up for them. Am I operating with my core values leading the way? Or am I missing the mark? If the yoga studio didn't pivot and offer the practice sessions the next morning, what feedback would we have gotten? In this next practice it is important to identify five people that you would like to provide the questions to. It is a mini survey that you can send out and simply let people know that you are seeking their input on how you show up in the world through their perspective. It is easy to send the questions to people you know that will be *nice* and not want to *hurt your feelings*. Instead, I invite you to take the challenge and send the questions out to a variety of people. Especially the ones where you find yourself saying, they don't know what they are talking about. The individuals where you find yourself getting defensive, those are the ones where there is likely the largest learning opportunity and the biggest chance for growth. You want to ensure you ask people for their honest and candid feedback. When they respond openly and truthfully, it will provide you with the space to grow.

QUESTIONS TO ASK:

You can ask all questions, or you can choose five questions that you want to receive unfiltered feedback on. Remember the intention of this practice is to understand how you are showing up in the world through the eyes of another person. This is very different from the filter of your own eyes.

1. What are my three strongest characteristics?
2. What are three things about me that drive you crazy?
3. What am I doing when you see me at my best?
4. What am I doing when you see me at my worst?
5. What can you count on me for?
6. What can you not count on me for?
7. When do you see me most inspired?
8. What was your first impression of me? What was it that gave you that impression?
9. Is there anything you would like to tell me that I did not ask?
10. If you had one wish for me what would it be?

The entire purpose of this practice is to get to the real deal before we begin to pivot, shift, or make any movement. This practice allows us to understand the impact that we have and don't have on others. It is an opportunity to bring our blind spots to life, to confront where we have made the mark in matching our intention with our impact, and also where we have missed the mark. I often find myself in a situation where I am speaking with my team about a guest experience and the team member will say, "well that wasn't my intention" and while I understand that it wasn't their intention, we often forget that it doesn't matter what we think we meant, the only thing that matters is how someone else experienced us. The guest's experience of us is the test, not the delivery. All we have is how someone feels their experience was of us. So no matter what your intention is, if the other person did not experience you in the way in which you intended, your actions and intentions are misaligned, and you are left with a choice. You can realign them, or not. That is the choice you are left with, and as we stated before, every choice has a possibility and a consequence.

PRACTICE 3

Brain Dump to Create Space

Every Sunday I found myself beginning the day carefree and whimsical and ending it stressed and overwhelmed. Sunday evenings I am often in the pattern of wondering: *what do I have to accomplish this week? What meetings do I have? Where do I need to be? Where do the kids need to be? What equipment do they need for hockey? Who's taking them to chess? To school? What's for dinner this week?* The barrage of questions and statements is never-ending and always going on Sunday evenings. I couldn't think fast enough and certainly not write fast enough to capture even a portion of what I would call a to-do list. What I found was that there was no room for me to think, brainstorm, or really do anything else. I was finding myself on a constant hamster wheel of things to do that really did not need to take up space in my thoughts. So I began to write everything down, all of it, as a practice to empty out my head and give myself the permission to forget it all because it was captured down on paper. It didn't matter if I remembered what specific thing I needed to do because I had written everything down.

That is the action that I want you to take right now.

BRAIN DUMP

On the following page write on each line all the things that are on your mind. It can be a thing to do, a project, a fear, an action to take, anything that you are holding on to that you have to remember and then do something about. Write everything down. Whether you are a new entrepreneur, a seasoned one, or an employee at a firm. What is on your mind that is held like a to-do, action, or future action? It is pertinent to write it all down without holding back. Allow yourself the time to take out all the things you have to remember.

Step 1: Write down everything in your head that you are holding as a to-do, or something to remember to take action on. Write one thing per line.

Step 2: Once you complete that you will categorize the list into three sections.

S–for scheduling it. This item needs to be done and I need to put it into my calendar.

D–for don't schedule it. Yes it needs to be completed but not now. It is not a priority and now that I have written it down I can take it off my mind, but right now it is not urgent.

N–for never doing it. These items write the letter N and cross it out. These are items that you are simply not doing, and never will, so you need to stop thinking about them and holding on to any guilt around not doing it. After all, your intention is to never do it.

To-Do   S/D/N

——————————————————————————————   ———

——————————————————————————————   ———

——————————————————————————————   ———

——————————————————————————————   ———

——————————————————————————————   ———

——————————————————————————————   ———

——————————————————————————————   ———

——————————————————————————————   ———

——————————————————————————————   ———

——————————————————————————————   ———

——————————————————————————————   ———

——————————————————————————————   ———

——————————————————————————————   ———

——————————————————————————————   ———

——————————————————————————————   ———

——————————————————————————————   ———

——————————————————————————————   ———

——————————————————————————————   ———

——————————————————————————————   ———

By creating space it allows us the opportunity to intentionally fill it back up, to place things there that will make a fundamental difference in our lives. As we begin to shift and move with ease, we need to release any of the excess emotional and mental baggage we tend to hold on to that slows us down. The more we can be committed to emptying out, the easier it will be for us to shift from one direction to the other, or from one area of your life to the other. Start to wake up to the excess stuff that is holding you down. If you are saying you want to change and move, but then are unwilling to ask for feedback or emptying out your to-do list. Notice where what you say and the actions you take are misaligned. It is only when our actions mirror our words that miracles appear, and the appearance of miracles in your life is completely and entirely up to you!

Week Two:
INTUITION

"There is a voice that doesn't use words.
Listen." -Anonymous

There are so many times I have done the complete opposite of listening to my intuition. I have simply shut it down and shut it out. I often wonder what it is that has me stop, disengage, and do the exact opposite? My wedding day would have been one of the most impactful moments of following my intuition, though I didn't know it at the time. It is only from the person I am today that I can share this story. You see, I was a young bride at the age of twenty-four marrying someone who bestowed all of the values I wanted for my future family. He was dedicated to his religion, great with his mom, and easy on the eyes. Mostly he was kind to everyone all of the time. We decided on a destination wedding before it was hip and popular. Against all opinions and judgements we headed off to Mexico to be married on the beach. I was expecting it to be the most joyous occasion, in a beautiful location celebrating with people near and dear to my heart. Well slowly things began to change. People who were definitely in for the wedding in Mexico suddenly began canceling one by one. The friends responsible for my husband and I meeting could no longer join us. We quickly realized that it would be an intimate wedding with simply our parents and a few key family members. At the time there were so many emotions, so many thoughts, and even more disappointment, but it wasn't until the night before our wedding that things really blew up and I would face a clear choice to pivot. A choice I didn't realize at the time was presented by my intuition. Intuition is not the ability to see the future, it is the opportunity to be one with shifts as they show up, and naturally flow through them. Sometimes we simply do not realize that there is a natural flow of life—the way a river flows downstream. Intuition is often misunderstood and ignored. In my case, things happened so fast I had no choice, but to go with the flow.

I come from a family with mental illness, each diagnosis has ranged from anything from schizophrenia to bipolar to depression. While in my early twenties, my younger brother began to battle with schizophrenia, although at the time we had no option and did not understand the severity of the disease and the impact it was about to have on our family. The night before my wedding my brother's illness reared its ugly head. I am still not clear on the exact details other than he got into a severe fight at our resort in Mexico that the police became involved, and if it wasn't for my soon to be husband's ability to speak Spanish and explain that my brother was ill and didn't mean the things he said or actions he made, he would have been incarcerated. My intuitive flow was on that night. I knew that even though I wanted my father to walk me down the aisle the next morning and for my family to be by my side as I married my life long partner, it was not the right decision for my family and more importantly for my brother for them to stay in Mexico; they immediately had to go home to get the proper care. The next day we gave what little money we had to my parents to purchase one way tickets home to Toronto. My destination wedding had turned out to be a nuisance and inconvenience to those I loved most. Suddenly I was flooded with the burden I had become and the selfish act of a destination wedding. The next few hours turned out to be another critical moment in my life and at the time it was no big deal. I am not sure whether I made the decision to carry on with the wedding out of guilt or absolute assurance that this was what I was meant to do. I do however realize looking back that I have the ability to create the narrative for every single situation, experience, and thought in my life; my narrative changes according to my mood, audience, and the reaction I am seeking. I could share the above and be the victim in it all or I could share the above from a place of compassion and question what was the impact on my family to miss such a day? Or another alternative I could share the story from the place of absolute confidence that I decided to continue on with the wedding from my heart, my intuition, and from the belief system of: what is meant for me will never skip me. The next day I would find myself alone, getting ready for my wedding with strangers. That day I let go of everyone's opinions, thoughts, and my concern for others' feelings, and instead I listened to the gentle whisper of my heart that guided me to marry my partner. I followed my intuition and allowed it to make the final decision that day. It is here that we will begin our exercise.

PRACTICE 1

Releasing Regret

What is regret? Regret is often a sad emotion or disappointment over something that did or did not happen. A missed opportunity or a loss. Something that simply did not go your way. Often we do not take the time to look at and process our regrets. This is an important step as you shift from one project, task, relationship to the other. If you want to avoid consistent patterns, we must take the time to acknowledge any past regrets.

For this practice you will need your journal (or use the page provided on page 45), a pen, and a timer. You can also use your phone and set a timer. Ensure that the timer has a gentle welcoming tone when it goes off. Set the timer to four minutes. While the timer is going you will close your eyes and think about everything you wished you had done in your life. As you do that I want you to imagine that each of the wishes, should haves, if onlys are placed on a raft. A very basic raft, the type Huckleberry Finn rode down the Mississippi River. Now imagine that the river flows in between both of your ears. The image is coming in through your left ear and then flowing out of your mind through your right, notice the repetitive act, notice what is on the raft, and notice how your body reacts to it all. Allow the flow to repeat over and over until you hear the timer chime. Once the timer chimes, open your eyes and pick up a journal.

Using another four minutes, on a fresh page list all of the regrets you visualized, thought about, or saw on the rafts—this is your Releasing Regret List. Journal answering these points:

- I wish I . . .
- I should have . . .
- If only . . .
- I could have . . .
- I regret . . .

Journal until you hear the timer; Even if you find yourself staring at the page. Notice if you are not writing because you don't want to relive or be reminded of your *misses*, or what you view as missed opportunities.

This practice is the one that took me the longest to write for my own experiences, and it was because I was having such negative body sensations. I had wished I had the courage to write the book sooner; I was regretting not having a local wedding, so my brother could have attended. One that I found brought up the most emotion was, "I should have stayed home when my sons were young to be with them."

Whatever is showing up for you, write it down. It may not make sense, but by bringing it out in words and applying action to it, you are allowing yourself to release yourself from the grip it may or may not have on you. It may be a grip that you may or may not be aware exists. Continue to journal until your timer chimes once again.

PRACTICE 2

Categorizing Regret

Journaling on my regrets has me spinning into a whirlwind of daydreaming and wondering what could have been and where did I miss out? What could I have done differently—imagining who I could have been? The problem is the more we leave things to our imagination and sense of wonder, the deeper hole we find ourselves in. We make things up and envision things that would have never been there to begin with. So how do we stop ourselves from going down the rabbit hole? How do we ground ourselves and our mood as we journey through this practice of PIVOT?

In this next practice we will get concrete with what exactly we are regretting. Yes, we are going to relive it AGAIN. I invite you to do this exercise as many times as it takes for you to have no charge or emotion around "what you missed out on."

Step 1: Grab your *Releasing Regret List* that you created earlier.

Step 2: Go through your list and label things (C) for Career, (P) for Personal or Family, and (V) for Vocation. It is pertinent that you categorize each and everyone one of your regrets.

Step 3: Once categorization is complete count the number for each and write it beside your legend.
(C) _____ (P) _____ (V) _____

Step 4: Answer the following questions; What are you noticing here? Is there an area that you have a higher number of regrets? Is it even?

The power in this practice is clarity. Where in YOUR mind did you miss your expectations for yourself? And I want to emphasize YOUR because you place the unrealistic expectations on yourself. No one else does. Then our mind plays tricks on us; it lies to us all the time by altering our perception of reality. Our mind, or imagination, can make us think things that are not true. Fooling us into thinking there is something wrong or that we simply have not done enough. Our imagination pulls us down and we become a victim.

The time must come when playing the victim of regret no longer fits for us. No longer is it how we want to go through life or relive our memories. There is a distinct choice that you make: you are choosing a new way of being and acting. This is not a one time choice. It is a choice and commitment made repeatedly. Day in and day out.

Regret and the story we have about it can paralyze the strongest individual. By speaking and sharing about it, it no longer has a grip on us.

Release Regret List   C/P/V

_____   _____
_____   _____
_____   _____
_____   _____
_____   _____
_____   _____
_____   _____
_____   _____
_____   _____
_____   _____
_____   _____
_____   _____
_____   _____
_____   _____
_____   _____
_____   _____
_____   _____
_____   _____
_____   _____

(C) _____ (P) _____ (V) _____

CORE VALUES VERSUS REGRETS

Taking your list and your CPV legend: compare the areas; what do you want to do more of? What area do you want to do less of? Where should you be focusing your attention? What should you take your attention off of?

* * *

When you start to get the intuition you have to act, what do you stop? Are you willing to be a *citizen*—a part of, contributing to the earth? Or are you a *consumer*? Taking and using? Simply taking up space. Intuition is not the ability to see the future, it is the ability to flow with the present, naturally with ease and grace. When you are following your intuition everything is easy. It is a natural flow of life that we don't realize we block like a dam blocks the natural flow of a river.

Intuition is often misunderstood. Intuition is a natural dynamic, where your five senses are no longer the logic you bring forth to all your decisions. The intuitive flow is always within us, we tend to not listen. Our default is to be the survivor and move into survival mode. This is often the solar plexus (third chakra), you don't have to awaken this intuition. The third chakra spins around our belly button and up to below our breast bone and it is known to support growth in confidence and vitality. It empowers you to follow your true path and create the life you want. When the **solar plexus chakra** is in balance it allows you to seize your personal power, develop your authentic self, and take responsibility for your life. We base our decisions on our spiritual intuition, whether we think we do or not. Even the most practical type A individuals are using their intuition to form the bases of their initial decisions. What happens after that is we use our rational thinking to take over because we cannot decide with our heart or intuition, that would not be right according to traditional thinking. When we use our rational thinking (five senses) we respond to life versus creating it with our intuitional decision.

You always develop an intuitive decision before you develop a physical (rational) one, so some have an opportunity to mature our intuitive ability. Our intuition is the direct polar opposite of our egos. There are many names that could be used for our ego—such as inner critic, saboteur, superego; and the opposite being for our intuition—inner wisdom, north star, and your truth. Just pick the term that works best for you. Your ego is the part of you that wants you to look good, to be liked, be successful and fit in to name a few. Your ego actively goes out of it's way to avoid fear and ensures that you always feel safe. Your intuition, as mentioned in this practice, is your inner wisdom, the part of you that knows what you truly want and need and just wants you to feel at peace. I think of it as the gentle whispers of my heart. Your intuition has a softer voice than your ego, and it can be easily ignored.

Over time, if you are not listening, your intuition will start to make a fuss and you'll have more internal resistance about where you are in your growth / life. You'll have a strong longing or feeling that you need to be doing this other thing, but your ego is going to justify reasons why that doesn't make sense. That feeling isn't going to go away until you start trusting and listening to your intuition. We often collapse our intuition with ego—for example, someone is acting a certain way around you, your ego has you thinking things like, *they are mad at me, they don't want to be with me, etc.* Yet we hear people say things like, *intuitively I know they have a problem with me, they don't like me.* That isn't their intuition, it is their ego being triggered by looking bad.

Change happens, endings and beginnings are normal and should be anticipated. We are looking to enter into a new flow of intuition with the intention of tapping into creativity. Shifting your attention from poor me to the manifestation of, yes I can, everything is possible, I will be creative. Simply making the declaration and controlling the shift will allow for new possibilities to open up that weren't going to happen naturally. You can go from sad one day to happy the next; to having no ideas at work to having all the ideas. The only way to experience this is to become mindful of your intuition.

Are you the type of individual that needs to understand everything that is happening? Are you able to accept the unexplainable? Consider that you have a choice on how you will react. The importance to creative flow is key in experiencing a new way. One that you could have never imagined or predicted. Catch yourself when you make decisions based on your ego or fear versus creativity or intuition; if you subconsciously choose fear over creation, to not listen to your intuition, and perhaps stay inside of a concept, we call this the drama triangle where you continue to stay trapped in fear.

Later on in the book we will explore the concepts of the drama triangle and look at where we create recurring patterns in our life that repeat with different characters and situations, yet the underlying mood remains the same. In the meantime can we begin to remove *coincidence* from your vocabulary? Can you accept that there is no luck or happenstance? Can we take accountability for us being responsible for everything that happens and does not happen in our life?

* * *

Sunday March 15, 2020, is the day that the act of being RESPONSIBLE and ACCOUNTABLE became more than clear, it was shouting to me. TAKE CONTROL. It is the day we pivoted for what we thought would only be fourteen days of closures due to some looming virus that had begun in Wuhan, China. You may have heard of it? The COVID-19 pandemic caused by the coronavirus. Yes, kind of a big deal. Little did we, or anyone else for that matter, know we were actually pivoting away from our existing comfortable business model into a model we had no idea would become our new normal. The practices of PIVOT are no longer a concept or something experienced on a small scale. Nope, there are no luxuries in the new world called COVID, where social distancing is the new normal. The practices became our daily tools.

Decisions are consciously made with the distinct question: (one) do you want to follow our core values? or (two) do you want to drive profit? The post COVID-19 landscape is still rolling out, it is not complete and in some ways it hasn't even started. There are many philosophies out there, many conspiracy theories. I have my own, and I hope you have yours. Why? Because it is important as you shift and alter that you stay awake and aware, and you question everything. That is the most powerful weapon that you have in your Pivoting Tool Kit. The ability and need to question it all. To look around and to wonder, what is happening. Very distinct from following the herd.

Sunday March 15, 2020, was the day we decided we had to close down our yoga studios. I distinctly remember taking my business partners class and convincing one of our teachers to stay back and practice with me.

"Where are you rushing off to?" I asked her. "Let me roll out your mat next to mine." This was my next statement, and that is what we did. We practiced yoga. In a class that normally had ninety participants, I found myself in a room with maybe thirty people. Social distancing had begun, despite there being no formal language around it. Hockey games and seasons had screeched to a halt, and in a land where you schedule your life around your kids and other kids' schedules, many of us were scrambling to understand and we questioned everything. What the heck was happening here? But it was that Sunday that our biggest PIVOT yet would happen. In less than twelve hours we decided to shift from our bricks and mortar model of physical space to our free live-stream on Instagram and Facebook. Followed by a membership based model online studio. Let me be clear: essentially we decided to go from a business making money, to a business serving people and giving back for free, to an online for profit business, all inside of fourteen days.

We all witnessed it; government shutdown of non-essential services; the closure of restaurants with your only option being take-out; and the shift in grocery store shopping experience where X marked your spot to wait outside the store to grab your items. Allowing people in one by one to ensure the practice of social distancing, and mitigating the Coronavirus from jumping onto you from another who can go undetected due to no symptoms or lack of opportunities to be tested. Everything was changing and, in my opinion, will continue to do so. We simply have to choose. Who do you want to be in the change? How do you want to show up? What will your legacy be in our time spent in our homes with our closest people? Or at least who we thought about being our closest people. Not all things, relationships, and businesses will survive. Nothing will look the same. COVID-19 is teaching us a strong lesson that humankind forgot. It is very simple and very easy to forget: *Don't get too attached, nothing stays the same.*

In this time of transitioning from pre COVID-19 to post COVID-19, and not really having an understanding of what post

COVID-19 looks like, it was clear that we, including our team, needed to start to co-create, make decisions, and choices together. What decisions do you know in your intuition you need to make and you keep pushing aside for another day? For me, Sunday March 15th was a day I had no choice but to make a decision, in my heart. There was always the decision to shut down the studios or wait until the government mandated us to do that.

Do you find yourself waiting for others to tell you what to do? To force your hand or to give you no choice? What pauses you on following your intuition? Your heart? Your deepest desires? Is it fear? Is it a failure? Is it a combination of the two? What could things look like or feel like if you did not allow fear and failure to drive your decisions? What if you were willing to start from ground zero? If all else went away would you be able to look at yourself in the mirror and be with the person you have been? Or did you spend so much time taking care of and pleasing others you did nothing for yourself. *Why do you pay your ego and keep your heart at bay?* That is a question that COVID-19 pulled out of me in March of 2020 at the very beginning of the pandemic. What would have happened if I allowed my ego, or *thinking brain*, to steer me where it thought I needed to go? Versus following my intuition of serving.

In the face of the pandemic we weren't concerned whether our business would survive being shut down. The question we had came from our heart and intuition, how can we support people through fear of quarantine if they can't access yoga? The toughest part of this for type A's is to do what you think you should do, not where your intuition is taking you. That is until we silence the brain just enough to hear the gentle whispers of our heart. The whispers so faint you can only hear them when you are still and listening. Pre COVID-19 it was impossible to hear while everyone and everything was running from one place to the other. Post COVID-19 it is impossible to hear anything else but your intuition. Mother nature banished us all to our rooms to think about what we have done and all the selfish choices we have made driven by ego and by money.

All of a sudden the entire world is swept with the same gift. The gift that all of us claimed to have none of and no one has been able to recreate, copy, or mass produce. We were all given the gift of *time*. What we did with it, how we spent it, and who we spent it with was all up to us. It was all our choice. We were suddenly confronted with the choice of will you be a citizen, contributing to the community or will you be a consumer, taking and using resources you don't need?

In the next practice, we will explore if you are a citizen or a consumer within various aspects of your life and will see what you choose to do moving forward.

PRACTICE 3

Permission to Choose

1. Are you a citizen in your life, work, and relationships? Or are you consuming? Explain when and where if you feel things vary.

_____

_____

_____

_____

_____

_____

_____

_____

2. Are you living life or are you trying to figure it out? In what areas?

_____

_____

_____

_____

_____

_____

_____

_____

_____

3. Knowing that there is no wrong answer, what space are you operating in?

- **CONSUMPTION**—taking up time, space, and resources.
- **CHOICE**—allowing for pathways to emerge and being creative.
- **COMPASSION**—being patient and allowing for heart whispers, and releasing fear.

Career: _____

Love: _____

Friendships: _____

Self: _____

Other: _____

4. Can you approach from a neutral place, with zero judgement?

Career: _____

Love: _____

Friendships: _____

Self: _____

Other: _____

Remember, you have choice and the whole purpose of life is to discover things along the way. No matter which path you take you can't go wrong if you are willing and able to be responsible and accountable for your actions and, more importantly, listen to the gentle whispers of your heart. The freedom to choose no matter the circumstances have always been with us. Plainly put, we never had control and the choice on how to react has always been ours. Choose wisely.

Week Three:
VISION

Week Three: Vision

"The only thing worse than being blind is having sight with no vision." -Helen Keller

Growing up before iPads, home computers, and TikTok, I remember spending countless hours creating dance shows in my parents' basement. I would organize every single detail from the choreography, to the music, to the style of my hair, and the outfit I wore. Using items found around the house to put on a full production during every family holiday gathering. I was clear those years of the exact end result I was working towards and would spend every extra moment to put the plan together. I didn't know it then, but I was very simply creating a vision for myself to live into. That childhood ability to be creative and to share what it is we are looking to enroll others into, is a gift that we all had at some point in time and slowly it starts to diminish and in some cases disappear. Our ability to imagine, day dream, and then share with others becomes something that we hold close to our chest without the willingness to open up to others. There is a short poem by Jack Gilbert that asks, *"Do you have the courage to bring forth the treasures that are buried deep within you?"* I would add: and are you willing to share and enroll others into them? When you are pivoting, it is not enough to simply turn around. The power and sustainability is the ability to pivot with a vision and the ability to share the vision with others. If you cannot share your vision, you simply have an idea. Ideas are great, they can be hashed out with others and bounced around, but they are not a vision.

When we first opened up our yoga studio, we had a very clear vision to teach Hot Power Yoga. That was it. The simplicity of the vision made it easy to communicate and to enroll others into it. It also was the thing that frustrated people the most; the wanting of us to expand to other styles and types of yoga; the need of others wanting variety. It just wasn't for us. We wanted simply to only teach Hot Power Yoga, so that is what we did.

For the purpose of this book, let's define vision as the ability to think and plan about the future and enroll others into it. In order to do this, we need to look at our ability to make, listen, and explore visions. As human beings we have the gift of thinking and inventing; we are constantly creating. How many of us have a business idea or a project that we haven't made public or even told a soul about? Ideas get in the way of creating a vision because our fear of "we are not good enough" or "no one will buy" is so loud that it is all we hear. We would rather listen to someone else's idea and complain about how that was our idea and they copied it, than take the action ourselves. What is holding us back in our ideas—in fine tuning it into a vision? What does it look like to begin the mining of ideas to cultivate a vision? In order to understand vision, let's clarify the distinction of vision versus opinion. A *vision* according to the dictionary is: the ability to think about or plan the future with imagination or wisdom. An *opinion* according to the dictionary is: a view or judgment formed about something, not necessarily based on fact or knowledge. Now let's take this example back to what I shared earlier about our vision with Power Yoga Canada to offer Hot Power Yoga—that was the vision (and that is what we were able to stick to for over a decade). Now other people definitely had the opinion that we may be missing out on the opportunity to grow our business by diversifying into other types of yoga such as yin, prenatal, etc. In those moments we had an opportunity to adjust our vision to accommodate their opinions or not. We simply had to make a choice.

There are fundamental elements of both visions and opinions and they both look very similar. It is quite often that we collapse opinions and visions together. We have seen that recently with companies like Starbucks. Their original vision was to offer the best cup of coffee in your second home. Later, they received the opinion or feedback of others that they should offer food, and so they ventured off to execute on others' opinions deviating from their original vision. Did it work? Was it a good deviation? Only Starbucks would be able to answer that. Let's take a closer look at the distinction between the two:

Opinion	Vision
A speaker	A speaker
A listener	A listener
Making a statement	Making a statement
Can be factual or not	Often not proven at least in the conception phase
Makes no difference if others are enrolled into it or not	Is a story that has the ability to enroll others into it

The key element in a vision is the ability to share and communicate it with others. A vision is a picture you need to paint in a way that others can follow and recreate it for others. The challenge is cultivating a vision that has you pop out of bed in the morning with excitement.

PRACTICE 1

Waking Up to Possibility

The idea of pivoting a well designed vision will give you a life that is self-generating, constantly creative, and one that serves you physically, emotionally, mentally, and financially. If you had told me back in 2009 that I was going to open a yoga studio and within ten short years it would swell to over thirteen locations, I would have thought you were crazy. Little did I know that was in the realm of possibility. This is an example of the limiting belief system we have that ultimately holds us back from creating anything outside of our current knowledge. For any of you that have studied with the Landmark Forum you would be familiar with the concept of the *Pie of Possibility*. Commonly the small slices of the whole pie is broken down by:

1. You know what you know (YKYK). An example of this would be I know that I know how to speak english. What is an example for you of: *you know what you know?*

2. You know what you don't know (YKDK). An example of this would be I know that I don't know how to speak Mandarin. What is an example for you of: *you know you don't know?*

3. This next distinction is one that I added in, which is: you don't know what you know (DKYK). I stumbled on this distinction when people would ask me how did you enroll people into your vision? It was a skill I didn't realize that I had and therefore had no language to share how to do that with others. What is an example for you of; *you don't know what you know?* A hint would be to look to where you have a certain level of mastery that comes naturally and happens without you thinking about it.

4. The last and biggest piece of the Pie of Possibility is: you don't know what you don't know (DKDK). Here is where you can't provide an example because if you knew it, it wouldn't

belong here. What is most interesting is, we live our life making decisions from such a small piece of the pie when the endless possibilities actually live in the unknown. Can you think of something you know, that was at one time in the realm of, *you don't know what you don't know?* For me, becoming a yoga studio owner when I was in my twenties was definitely something in the unknown. In fact I did not even discover yoga until I was pregnant with my first son at the age of twenty-four.

PIE OF POSSIBILITY

In one of our recent training programs a student reminded me that this concept has ancient roots with Confucius:

> *He who knows not, and knows not that he knows not, is a fool—shun him.*
> *He who knows not, and knows that he knows not, is a child—teach him.*
> *He who knows, and knows not that he knows, is asleep—wake him.*
> *He who knows, and knows that he knows, is a wise man—follow him.*

The illustration of the pie of possibility demonstrates the complete blind spot that we live in the majority of our life. In the book, *Remembrance of Things Past*, Marcel Proust says, *"The true journey of discovery does not consist of searching for new landscapes, but in having 'new eyes'."* We live with our point of view completely off the larger piece of the pie, and worse, we give our opinions saying that the larger piece of the pie doesn't exist and kill off any vision or dream that we have for ourself—or worse yet, that others have. It becomes a vicious cycle where if we can't live out our dreams no one else can live out theirs. Where we can start to separate ourselves and really allow our intuition and gentle whispers of our heart to support us in our pivot is simply by looking at the observer that we are.

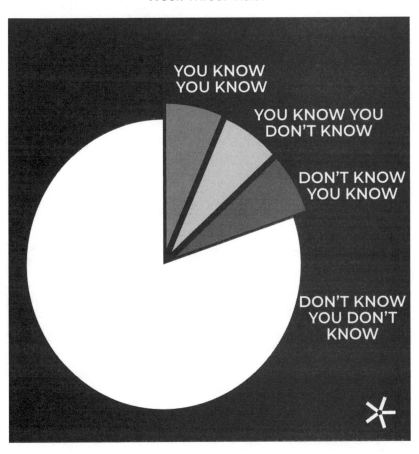

Exercise: Close your eyes and start to notice the ebb and flow of your breath. With your eyes closed can you begin to observe yourself? Can you start to be the witness to you and your actions?

PRACTICE 2

The Observer—You Are Your Point of View

Journal on the following questions:

1. What are you telling yourself when you observe yourself; what is your way of thinking?

2. Can you identify a situation where living and acting inside of the smaller piece of the pie has had you limited?

3. How does that thinking block you or stop you from gaining access to a new possibility? Where are you blocked?

4. What possibility would have you jump out of bed every morning?

5. How would you like to show up in your life for yourself, your family, or at your place of work?

6. How are you showing up?

7. What messes do you have in your life? With whom? About what?

8. Is there anyone or anything you need to forgive in order to continue to move forward?

Often we find ourselves brushing over things or sweeping things under the rug; ignoring and not making a *big deal* about anything. It is the unspoken that usually lingers and permits us from pivoting quickly and swiftly. When I find myself or a client stuck and unable to change and move, generally the place I need to look is: am I incomplete with myself or someone else? Do I need to forgive myself or another for something I did or for something I did not do? Forgiveness can be complicated or it can be very quick. That is completely up to you. The only caveat in all of it is that forgiveness must be genuinely given. It is not something that you can simply go through the motions. It must be meant and it must be felt. This next practice is optional and a great practice to refer back to at any point in your life.

PRACTICE 3

(Optional)

Forgiveness

This next practice is not for the faint of heart. You must be committed and interested in taking on your life in a whole new way to access a whole new level of possibility. This must be done with zero expectation of the outcome. The freedom here is only available when one is not attached.

Step 1: Set a serious intention to forgive and express the willingness to do so, especially if you have no idea on how you will get there.

Step 2: Add your willingness to forgive into a daily meditation.

Step 3: Begin reminding yourself that you were in this relationship or situation for a reason, and that you had a part in creating the dynamic that was happening. Look for where you need to take accountability in the situation.

Step 4: Remember taking accountability is distinct from taking responsibility for another person's harmful behavior. Can you question why you tolerated a situation?

Step 5: Be willing to forgive yourself and accept the learnings you have had on the way.

Step 6: Remember that forgiving yourself is the pathway to forgiving others. Choosing forgiveness allows you to close the lingering items of the past and opens new pathways for the future. It is from this place that you can begin to create your vision.

This exercise is a practice that you can do over and over again for the rest of your life. I can guarantee that in life you will disappoint yourself or another, and someone else will do wrong by you. The act of forgiveness is not a one time thing and often we think that it is for another person. However, the act of forgiveness is for yourself. You are not telling the other person you forgive them, you are not welcoming them back into your life. The person doing the forgiving is the one that is freed up to be in their full self-expression and create a vision in their life that is powerful and consistent with who they want to be in the world.

Throughout the years I have consistently begun each new year with a ritual of creating a manifestation collage to set a vision that I will live into the year ahead. This simple exercise has forced me to feel complete and finished with the past year. It includes forgiving myself for the things I did not complete and the places I missed the mark. At the same time it affords me the opportunity to acknowledge where I did hit the mark and accomplished what I set out to do. In the practice of creating a vision for you to pivot to, you must first get complete with the place you are pivoting from. The last exercise this week will be to create a vision for yourself. This can be a specific statement, a visual, or a letter that you write to your future self.

PRACTICE 4

Create Your Vision

While creating a vision could seem like a daunting task, questioning how do I even begin? Especially these days, at the time of writing this book we are finding ourselves quarantined in our homes making a future plan may seem like the most impossible task. It is when we are most challenged, that our best work comes out. To begin creating your vision do as many of the below steps as possible. People often leave out the first one, the collage because of the amount of work; I would argue that it is the most important one.

This last practice is to choose your own adventure, so choose wisely:

1. Create a vision board for yourself filled with images and words that speaks to you. You do not need to know how you will accomplish the things that you are putting down. In fact the less planned it is, the better. You will need the following:

   • Canvas or base sheet

   • Old magazines or picture books that can be cut up

   • Scissors

   • Glue

2. Write a letter as your future self. Close your eyes and visualize where you want to be in one year from now. Where are you living? What are you wearing? Who is with you? When you awake what will your day be like? Here's my example:

This was my two year vision letter written June 11th, 2018:

> *I woke up this morning and started my day working out with Gerard, part of our regular routine before we split off to get the boys to school. Today I am going to meet up with G mid-morning to complete our book and online workshops called, "It Takes Two." I am going to spend lunch meeting up with a potential new business opportunity. It is my favourite way to meet up with people—doing a workout and today it is the reformer. Gerard is loving life so much post plumbing career, and I am so glad that we get to spend our mornings together. Jacob is thriving in his new school and Noah has his eyes set on attending a NCAA College. I am planning to meet with our financial advisor to determine how best to continue to save for the boys' futures, and I am completing the purchase of our vacation home in Portugal and rental property in the city. This weekend I am traveling to deliver a keynote on "Thriving in your business" and giving away copies of "F@#$ Balance, Kill Hope and Get to Work."*
>
> *Meditation and prayer is at the foundation of who I am and have been practicing regularly with Gerard. This summer I am planning on taking the family to Asia exploring the Great Wall of China. Continuing to support my friend Paige with the Africa Yoga Project I am working closely with at-risk youth within the Greater Toronto Area. The words of Mother Theresa inform my being and acting; "If you want to change the world, go home and love your family."*

Once you have completed one or both exercises, journal on what you are seeing as a vision for yourself. Is there anything that surprised you? Are you satisfied with what you came up with and are you excited? Whatever you have documented should have you jumping out of bed. Our visions are also dynamic and not static. It's like you can shift, morph, and evolve over and over again. Everytime you pivot your vision comes along with you. It is important to stay fluid and awake to what you and your vision need to do, to fulfill your future self as your path changes and becomes more clear. Your vision will soon become the water flowing down the stream. The water always finds its way, willing to go with the flow facing every rock and obstacle it meets.

Week Four:
OBSTACLES

"In the middle of every difficulty lies opportunity." -Albert Einstein

When we had to shut down all the yoga studios due to COVID-19 hitting North America, it was as if we were living in a very bad dream. First off, it was not even in our realm of thinking this could be possible, it was in the realm of "we don't know what we don't know." Secondly, the business model as we knew it was over, gone, and dead. Will it come back? Eventually. But the real question is: will it ever be the same? Absolutely not. COVID-19 was a clear demonstration that we have no control over what happens. Everyone who claimed that the government had taken away our control didn't realize that control was not theirs to take away because it never existed anyways. Once again the only thing we were left with was the opportunity to choose our actions and reactions. There was a choice at that moment—a clear opportunity and fork in the road—and we had to choose one way or the other. Neither route was wrong and each route was distinctly different. We could have at that point closed the studios and put everyone's memberships on hold; one direction in the fork of the road. Or, we could have gone online and continue our offerings through another way. Again, another fork in the road that was simply a different choice.

Can you think of forks in the road on your path that will have you pivot? Do you take them? Do you acknowledge the other path? Or do you simply continue on your way? These forks in the road come up more than we realize. We sometimes live our lives like we have no choice, that we are prisoners to our past decisions, but we indeed have choices. We can take another way, but we have to be awake and present enough to see it, to allow it, and to make it happen.

That day we ended up pivoting and taking everything online. There were many obstacles and I took a completely paid model and made it available gratis. Whether that was the right move or not we still don't know, but it was the right decision for the citizens of our studios and for the citizens of our country. It was a decision that was following our intuition. The war and quarantine of COVID-19 was a pivot and a shift many people were not ready for, and I don't mean with supplies or toilet paper. For many it also wasn't a choice. Their false sense of control was eliminated with every governmental address. It was a mandate to sit and be at home. All of a sudden it didn't matter how important you were or how many meetings you had because you were not allowed to leave your home or go anywhere. The small act of getting groceries made its return to be the most exciting event of the week. Family dinners every night became the thing to do. I know in my household, rituals were brought in and cherished and all of a sudden we were forced to spend a lot more time together day in and day out. There are many philosophies out there of the origin of COVID-19 and the science behind it. I am not an expert nor do I have the credentials to say anything informative from that perspective. What I do know is that John Welwood coined the phrase "*Spiritual Bypass*" in 1984. He was essentially referring to using spiritual practices such as yoga, meditation, reiki, etc. (I would even consider general fitness) as a way to avoid dealing with our painful feelings and unresolved wounds and our development needs. Being the owner of a yoga studio brand with multiple locations, this really hit home. Have we been helping people and supporting them in their pathway or have we been an obstacle blocking their pivot—from dealing with what is actually happening in their life? I don't know the answer to that question, but the spiritual bypass concept quickly became right sized with the wave of the coronavirus that had no bias to age, race, or gender—and did not care if you did yoga or not. If you got sick, it would go one of two ways; you will recover or you will die. We are in the midst of no longer being able to hide in our spiritual bypass. The time to make choices and choose the fork and path we wish to walk is now here, and we have to be willing to face the obstacles head on. We can no longer afford to bury our head in the sand and wait till the storm is over because it is not ending, and we are a part of the storm.

Originally when I had the concept of this book, the obstacle that I wanted to reference in this chapter was leaving my international work to come home and be with my family. I had spent about five years traveling for at least six months each year. When I began this work, I had just had a baby. A growing family was not an obstacle for me, it was an opportunity. I made the choice to go with the flow and was committed to making it all work, and it did for a period of time. When it stopped working it became so clear to me; the travel was dreaded, I could barely pull myself up to pack my bags. I dreaded airports, hotel rooms, and eating out. Everything about it made me miserable, and I stayed in that misery for over eight months. I didn't have the courage to pull myself out of that hole, or maybe I didn't have the strength. In the end I left and didn't look back. And that is a pattern in my life. I wait until things are so bad I have no choice but to leave. When COVID-19 hit, it became clear that there was no right way, but rather different ways and that we had a very short window to make a choice, but we had to make the choice and live with it. I had never done that before, get in front of the choice and choose it before it chose me. It was a clear pivot that needed to happen: back then with my job; and that day in the shutting down of the studios. In each situation I was a completely different person. In the job, I was a victim; no one was listening to me, I wasn't aligned with the vision for the organization, blah, blah, blah. It's funny even writing about it now, it has no charge for me because it was a way I was choosing to be. I wasn't taking accountability for my role in it all, so all I did was allow for myself to be a victim and create something called a drama triangle. A theory created and taught by Dr. Stephen Karpman. Some of you may have seen this before.

There are three points in the drama triangle and every time you find yourself in a dramatic situation or encounter, you should pause and ask yourself what role am I playing here?

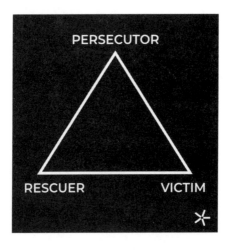

The three roles are as follows:

Victim: their core belief is "my life is so unfair, why do things keep happening to me."

Persecutor: "I'm surrounded by fools, idiots, or people less than."

Rescuer: "Don't fight, don't worry, let me jump in and fix everything."

These roles come up time and time again. When I was attempting to leave my job I was paralyzed in making a decision because I was so strongly playing the victim role and the rescuer role. At one point I finally made a decision to leave and submit my resignation letter and it wasn't accepted because I was so needed and had to fulfill my contract. Right at that moment I went into the rescuer role and was going to do right by the company and support them through everything. What quickly shifted was me moving into the victim role and becoming completely resentful and angry; I resigned because I was doing something I did not want to do and I didn't have the authority within myself to stick with a decision and see it through. In the case of pivoting our business online I was able to make a clear decision because none of those elements were at play. The decision was not based on fear nor was I fearful of the role I was playing in it. It was simply a fork in the road with a decision that had to be made.

PRACTICE 1

The Roles we Play

Looking at the model of the drama triangle journal on the following questions:

1. Think of a situation where the drama triangle was present in your life. What was the situation? With whom? About what?

2. What role did you play in the situation? Did your role shift? Did you notice it at the time or are you seeing if from the observer you are today?

3. Can you think of another time you were inside the drama triangle? Do you have a pattern of roles or behaviors?

Often times we say we are dedicated to our personal growth and evolution, but we are often unconsciously or intentionally not willing to look at what is causing the drama or repeated painful actions. Sometimes it is also our lack of accountability that allows the situation to linger, grow, and eventually cause more disruption than necessary. Instead of dealing with this we put in a spiritual practice or more self-care to avoid looking at the situation and things for which we need to be accountable. In order to pivot with flow and ease you need to take a hard look at the obstacle YOU ARE BEING FOR YOU. We can talk about all the things in your way, time, money, resources, but if we get to the bottom of it all the only thing stopping you is likely you and the role you play in it. The question is are you willing to drop your repetitive actions and ways of being to potentially allow you the space to choose a different path?

PRACTICE 2

Blocking Creativity

Now that we have addressed the biggest obstacle—you—and taking accountability for all of it, let's take a look at some other things that could be obstacles in your stream's flow. The large boulder being you and the smaller rocks are things that need to be addressed. Grab your journal and write a list of all the things that are in your way of creating. Obstacles that will make it harder or perhaps impossible to get done. Time, money, and people are the most obvious and often put down here. Take some time and jot down your list.

There are many things that support us in moving forward and growing, and there are obstacles that we ourselves continue to be or allow to block us. Notice if you were having a tough time writing down other obstacles that are in your way. Let's break down the Obstacles for Growth and Opportunities for Growth.

Obstacles for Growth:

- The inability to admit "I don't know."
- When you don't know what you don't know, but act as though you do.
- Confusion.
- Addicted to feeding the ego; boosting your self-importance in situations.
- Making *everything* important or (the opposite) unimportant.
- Addicted to being the hero.

Opportunities for Growth:

- Willingness to listen.
- Being Open.
- Ability to ask questions.
- Exercising curiosity.
- Takes accountability for actions.

There is a distinctly different way of being with growth and making the choice. I have seen what happens when I have made decisions from the place of, I know better or more. There will always be obstacles, but if you want to pivot with ease versus pivoting with force you have to take accountability for the drama, behaviors, actions, and non actions that you cause over and over again. If we want to shift the results that we are getting, we always have a choice. We can do nothing, and in our case of shutting down the studios we had that choice. Close and do nothing. We could take new actions, either physical actions or in our language. That is what we chose to do, we chose to offer free classes online, for a period of time.

Lastly you can take a look at the observer that you are. What is the point of view you are bringing to this situation? We discussed this in the vision practices during week three. Bringing the observer in allows for you to potentially make another decision. In the case of shutting down the yoga studios during the COVID-19 pandemic, when we stepped back and looked at the bigger picture we saw that there was a different way we could operate by taking our entire studio on to a virtual platform and delivering live interactive classes and monetizing that model. What do you see when taking the seat of an observer—when you remove yourself from the situation; what is the bigger picture, what are the other positive options and outcomes?

To summarize the actions to review when faced with an obstacle or opportunity for growth, and sometimes referred to as a fork in the road is as follows:

1. Do nothing—which in itself can be a very valuable tool.

2. Take a new action, in the form of physical or language.

3. Be an observer and look at things from a place of, you don't know what you don't know.

Reflecting on the way in which you view obstacles can allow for you to have a new relationship with them. Instead of obstacles being heavy and a burden, can you create obstacles as a part of the process and a way to grow and develop? If we can shift our point of view with obstacles, they all of a sudden become a part of the ecosystem and belong there. For example a stream of water flowing down does not view the rock as an obstacle, but rather a part of the journey downstream. It doesn't attempt to remove or change its place, rather it flows around it. Sometimes the journey around is much more complex and difficult, but the end result is the same; the water continues its flow downstream. The ecosystem has a way to work and flow as an entire unit. Some things win and stay around longer, but there is a natural ebb and flow of supporting the whole. Whether it is intentional or not.

PRACTICE 3

The Observer in Everyday Life

The last practice this week is quite simple. Get outside and take a walk. Be an observer out in nature. If you can walk near a creek or stream please do so with care and in complete observation of the way nature works together in collaboration and hand-in-hand. There is no posturing, no better than, and no hurtful conversations. Rather a commitment to the greater whole and an assurance that we will be committed to working together. As you walk around, what can you commit to reframing in your thought process in your way of listening, acting, and being? Where is there an opportunity for you to shift your perspective to get out of your own way? Is there repetitive drama triangle scenarios that you are looking to limit or simply be aware of?

The opportunity here with PIVOT in the practices of obstacles is quite simply to not remove them, but rather to work with them. Use the obstacles as a platform to reframe, redirect, and maybe even retool. What if obstacles became a part of the opportunity? When we shifted from a bricks and mortar model to an online model we were addressing a fundamental need for the business to close our studios due to a pandemic. One that was completely out of our control. There was no way for us to avoid it, we had to go with the flow. By not resisting it, it allowed us to pause and come up with a new business model that would survive the pandemic of COVID-19, and in fact allow us to grow our digital and international presence long after COVID-19 is gone. In these instances not controlling or holding onto the situation allowed for us to make informed decisions and act in a way to support everything and everyone.

Next week we will begin talking about the tactics that need to be taken. For now, can you keep your attention on who you need to be in order for the pivot to occur or not occur? What type of mood do you need to be in? What environment do you need to cultivate? Do you need to be curious? And most importantly can you land on the accountability that you are for yourself?

Week Five:
TACTICS

"The pessimist complains about the wind; the optimist expects it to change; the realist adjusts the sails."

-William Arthur Ward

As we enter into the last week of our *PIVOT* program, I tend to see the highest level of unease amongst the group. There are usually three different reactions. There is the eager individual that has it all figured out and can't wait to get started. They usually say things like, "I can't wait to get to writing my blueprint, so I can put this all into play!" Then there is the analytical individual who is looking at all the probable ways that things could work or not work and challenges that may come up along the way. They usually say things like, "Have you considered? Did you look at . . . " and "I am not sure, but maybe we can shift and pivot." Lastly there is the never doing it individual. They usually say things like, "This is never going to work, I am just going to stick with what I know." Inside they are fearful and their fear has taken control and hijacked the amygdala part of their brain. The amygdala is the filing cabinet of the brain; it is where we store our memories and events so that the emotions such as anger, fear, and sadness may be recognized and reappear when we see a similar situation arising. Flight or fight response has kicked in, and they are choosing to take flight. If pivoting was easy, everyone would do it. I even see people take on all three positions in the same conversation. Even today as I write this chapter I am processing the reactions of my husband choosing to leave his plumbing job of twenty plus years to be home with the children. All these emotions are surfacing and if you read my two year vision letter in chapter three, you would know him leaving his job was a part of my vision. I am eager for the change and excited to plan; worried and nervous, wondering if we are doing the right thing; fearful because this new way is unknown, how is it going to look? Similar to the drama triangle only this time it is whether we have the willingness to act and not be attached to whether we win or lose. The over analysis can also leave us in extreme paralysis; completely shutting down our ability to create, move, and mobilize.

In this final week it is pertinent that you keep moving forward. Forward motion is the name of the game. Regardless as to what you decide to do, there is no going back, it is impossible, the past has already happened and you cannot go there. It will always be something new, so catch yourself when you hear yourself saying, "I wish things could go back to how they used to be," or "Why can't things just stay the same?" Change isn't coming, it's here. Nothing will ever be the same because it simply cannot be. You will never have all the exact same circumstances, reactions, or results because of the simple fact that you and your life is not a rerun of *Friends*. In fact, even your reaction of watching the rerun of *Friends* or your favorite television show will never be the same. You might notice something you didn't notice before and find it hilarious or silly. You, the person watching the rerun, are not the same person and therefore you cannot be the same.

This week it is crucial that you watch your words and language, but most importantly your habits. Are your old ways of being kicking in? Are you resisting the need to move and pivot? Are you looking to keep things the same? Well there is no same, same does not exist unless you are playing the memory game and looking for the match card. In this entire COVD-19 crisis the number one thing I have heard from fellow business owners has been: "I can't wait until we get to go back into our business, and open up again and get back to normal." I just want to scream every time I hear someone say "back to normal." What is the definition of normal? How can you return back to what you considered normal? Right now social distancing is the new normal. Arriving at a grocery store and leaving six feet in between you and another individual to line up OUTSIDE the grocery store, so that you can safely practice social distancing in a 100,000 square feet grocery store is normal. Masks are mandatory, temperature checks before essential workers clock in for work is required, health checks before boarding a flight for domestic travel—this is the new "normal" and no one would have predicted any of this sixty days ago. If we can learn to go with the flow we can pivot with grace and ease and navigate through the constantly changing waters, which is what nature has intended for us to do, but "normally"—in the past—we simply have been comfortable with the status quo. Comfortable, until we are not, until we shift, disrupt, and force ourselves to pivot. The tools and practices we have been speaking about over the last few weeks are not a one-time phenomenon; it is a repetitive thing. It is a forever practice. The way I view my yoga practice is the way I view my practice of pivot. It will happen again and again. Everytime I get comfortable and say, "I can do this, I can be here for a while like this," something changes. There is a shift and a movement that has me reconsider everything I wanted to "stay the same." The COVID-19 circumstances forced us to quickly get up to speed on what was available online, and forced our yoga studios to become familiar with the likes of virtual video platforms and responding to social media messages instead of welcoming people into our brick and mortar classrooms. It was a steep learning curve with finite resources and time. *How do we conduct ourselves online? How do we create the energy online while our viewers have distractions at home and virtually?* Most people went into organizing their drawers and upping their Netflix intake. We went to work, countless hours; testing models, proving models, and then changing models every two weeks. Why? because that is how quickly things were changing. One week people are angered that they have to stay home, the next week they are devastated because the death toll keeps rising, and then it shifts to upset again with the danger of going to the grocery store. All of these are simple shifts and the opportunity to be awake to what is happening in the world and then protecting yourself, your business, and your family from going with the trend. The thing that has supported our business for the last decade is simply being awake to what it looks like to be with people and to not be influenced by everyone. I would say to my business partner, "Put your horse blinders on." Make a plan, work the plan, and measure the results.

In the time of COVID-19, I kept my family quarantined from the quarantine. Meaning I wanted us to stay informed and protect ourselves from the barrage of news, theories, and fake news that one could easily consume. It was very important to protect ourselves and limit what we brought into our personal space. This is not a new practice. This is a practice that we have done at Power Yoga Canada for years. We could not be everything to everyone, so we weren't. You won't make decisions that will satisfy everyone's opinions, so don't. The concept of pivoting and shifting will not be for everyone. And for those of you it is for, other people will question and wonder why you are pivoting. Why in the world would you change your job when you have a perfectly good nine to five gig that pays well and has a great benefit package? Because you have been called to grow.

When we were discussing the idea of opening up a yoga studio back in 2009, my mother was perplexed and puzzled as to why I would leave a strong corporate job with a car allowance and great benefits to take a chance and open up a yoga studio. Back then I wasn't worried about the stability of income or the retirement plan. What I was looking for was to fulfill my need to have my skill set challenged and recognized, and to jump head first into the unknown. There was the combination of the gentle whispers and calculated business plan with a clear model. It was the perfect storm of planning, passion, and a whole whack load of sweat equity. There are no guarantees that your pivot or shift will work out perfectly, just as equally there are no guarantees that you will know what to do with the new found success you may find, or that may find you. All we could do back in 2009 was keep moving forward. You must gain the muscle to act and react. To make a decision and follow that decision until you need to pivot again.

With Power Yoga Canada we learned to take an action and shift and alter on the fly. To get moving and then alter as needed. No different than the practice of yoga. The most challenging thing is to get onto your mat. To convince yourself to get going: to roll out that mat and step on it. Once you get moving, you very rarely see people leaving yoga classes half way through. Once they have made it over the initial hump of walking through our doors, it is pretty much a 99 percent guarantee they will complete that class. The same would go for getting to the gym, once you scan your membership card, it is unlikely that you will leave without completing some type of workout. What is the thing that you will need to do in order to make it over your hump? When we start to understand and be present to things that trip us up, it becomes easier to call ourselves out and hold ourselves accountable. This is the perfect time to move into practice number one this week.

PRACTICE 1

What Must be Present

In the spirit of preparing ourselves to pivot and take on new habits, what are some of the things that you need to stop doing? Things that are either no longer of value or relevance in the new direction that you are taking? Or ending relationships with people you need to stop being around. Grab your journal and write out all of the things you need to stop doing at home, work, and play.

One of the basic tactics to fulfill your vision is going to be your requirements, or the things that you will need to do. Once you are complete with all of the things you want to *stop* doing, we need to determine what are the things you *will* do. A requirement is something that you absolutely have to do or have it happen in order for your pivot to work. Requirements tend to be non-negotiable and the absence of a single one would have you feeling like you failed or something is wrong.

Requirements tend to have the following characteristics:

1. They are non-negotiable and become your word to yourself. If they were missing your pivot would not work.

2. They tend to be black or white, met or not met, there is normally not much room for grey.

3. Although they are black and white, they are also subjective, meaning it is your standard and not someone else's. For example with PYC a requirement is heat (for hot yoga), by our standard. You do not need heat to do yoga, but for PYC it is an important element.

4. They tend to come up very easily. If you have to think about it, you won't do it; so save yourself from feeling like a failure and don't write it down if it isn't important to you.

The flip side of requirements is *needs*. Now, a need often gets confused with a requirement. Needs are nice to have and are feel-good things whereas requirements are a must. Needs can be physical needs, and consider them to be functional, like I need a new MacBook Pro to become a famous writer. Well do you really? A need can be emotional, for example, I need my partner to be one hundred percent aligned and in love with my new direction. Again, nice to have, but do they really? A requirement might be that they are supportive of you, but you don't need them to believe in your idea.

The other thing that often gets misinterpreted are *wants*. Wants provide sheer pleasure and enjoyment. For example, I want to make a lot of money. Wants can be important for our quality of life, but it could be a mistake to base a pivot or decision based on wants since they are solvable and can change frequently and rapidly. Missing the mark on a want is solvable, missing a requirement could result in a failed pivot.

PRACTICE 2

Forming Habits

Let's take the time now to dive into the three categories and outline what are our requirements, needs, and wants. We need to identify these in order to understand what habits have helped or hurt us and what new habits do we need to create? Take a fresh sheet of paper and what you will write is about when you pivot and shift directions. These are the basic requirements, needs, and wants that you must have in order to feel like you are winning. Notice that I am not directing this to a specific pivot. These are going to be fundamental and universal things that you have put in place every time you pivot. The plan here is to use this as your template and not have to recreate it every time, although things will shift and change so this list will morph as the years go by. Essentially this will become your list of things that supports your life working.

Requirement	Need	Want
Non-negotiable feelings or things to be able to pivot.	Nice to have or feel good things. Could be either physical or emotional.	Provide sheer pleasure or enjoyment.

Once you have completed your lists review them and ensure that you have captured everything that you want to be listed. Review and edit as many times as you need.

Back in week three we spoke about the importance of having a vision; a clear direction for where you are heading and what you are up to. Often in the corporate world you will have organizations that have a clear mission, vision, and values statement or blurb on their website. They tend to collapse into each other and the other tendency is they are often forgotten. With Power Yoga Canada the *Mission* is to empower communities into action. Our *Vision* is to live our core values everywhere in our lives which are: speaking straight, listening generously, honoring our commitment, being for each other, and acknowledgment and appreciation. Our *Purpose*, or why we exist is to be the best in delivering Hot Power Yoga. Whenever we are looking to make a move or pivot with PYC we always look to our MVP (Mission, Vision, Purpose) to guide our decision. This can be done for a business no matter size or number of people, and can also be done for an individual person for their personal life. Creating your personal MVP gives you a framework and a place to stand from. It allows you to clearly stand in who you are and who you are not. If we stand for nothing we will easily fall for everything.

Now more than ever it is important to make the choice. To choose and be for what you want to see happen. It also starts to put accountability on yourself for how you want to show up in the world. Do you want to be a consumer or do you want to be a contributing citizen? You get to make that choice in writing and creating your personal MVP and driving your blueprint.

As you shift directions, sometimes a clearly written out plan is required to know exactly where you want to go. Sometimes, all you need is a framework and guidelines to lightly show you the way to shift, turn, and navigate through the ebbs and flows of the ecosystem we call life.

As we roll into our final practice, where can you add ease and play to the creation of it all? Can you be gentle with yourself and build the new muscle of ease and flow through transition and change? What if we saw change as a constant—as a welcomed element in the storms of life? What if we shifted our point of view of storms in general? The new perspective that we are speaking about here is forming new habits. New habits are a powerful place for me to be within the midst of the COVID-19 storm; there were consistent actions that I had not been taking that clearly needed to be added in. To see another perspective, another point of view, a way through the storm and not escaping it. There have been many storms in my life; the most vivid one I can remember was navigating through the development of my brother's schizophrenia, understanding the shifts that were happening and quickly learning what it all meant along the way—how we would navigate through this new normal, who I would be through it all. The habit I developed during that time as a coping and combatting solution was one of health and wellness.

You see, your MVP doesn't only guide you through your lightest hour, but also through your darkest. Through the times where you are not looking to build a thriving business, but rather survive dealing with a traumatic event or a devastating shift in a relationship with a loved one. Your blueprint guides you through every pivot and turn along the way. Whether you have forced it or it was forced on you. Change is always with us. It is up to us as to whether we allow it or resist it. Either way it is coming for you and you simply have to make your choice.

In the writing of this book I have further crystallized *my* MVP: My *Mission* is to empower other leaders around the world; My *Vision* is to live my core values of building, nurturing, and loving everyone and everything (especially the men in my life, Gerard, Noah, and Jacob); and my *Purpose* is to build over and over again.

PRACTICE 3: PART 1

Your MVP

Your turn! Write out your MVP. Don't make it complicated and don't over analyze it. Simply allow your heart to lead the way. This is food for your soul and your head does not need to understand it. Allow the gentle whispers of your heart to inform you here and now.

Is this MVP for business or personal? _____

Mission: _____
_____
_____
_____
_____
_____

Vision: _____
_____
_____
_____
_____
_____

Purpose: _____
_____
_____
_____
_____
_____

PRACTICE 3: PART 2

What are the NEW Habits?

What are three immediate actions that you need to take in order to begin your pivot? I would consider these to be new habits. Habits are done in repetition, over and over again, not a one time phenomenon. These are actions that you must do over and over again in order to achieve what you are looking for. You may not know exactly the direction, but you know there are three steps that need to be taken. Write them out now.

New Habits: _____

_____
_____
_____
_____
_____
_____
_____
_____
_____
_____
_____
_____
_____
_____
_____
_____
_____
_____
_____
_____
_____
_____
_____
_____
_____

PRACTICE 3: PART 3

My Team

Who do you need to enroll into this new way or direction? Who will be on your team? Who do you need to share your MVP with and enroll them into your overall vision? Write their names out now.

My Team: _____
_____
_____
_____
_____
_____
_____
_____
_____
_____
_____
_____
_____
_____
_____
_____
_____
_____

This blueprint becomes a very quick card as a reminder to point you back to what you stand for, what you need to keep your focus on, and who is on your team to support you along the way. There is nothing about pivoting that is easy, or at least it seems, but when we have all the support systems in place, we know we are able to accomplish the impossible and achieve extraordinary results.

The actions identified in this last week are meant to support you in finding ease and confidence to shift and navigate in whatever direction you find yourself heading. These days, we are learning that there is power in clear concise action that is targeted to reach certain people. If we all begin to take accountability for the results we obtained from the actions we put forth, I think we will begin to change the world.

Margaret Meade stated, *"Never doubt what a small group of committed citizens can do to change the world, in fact it is the only thing that ever has."* Decide who you want to be in your role here on the planet and then simply follow that through day in and day out. In the small experiences and the large ones. Create the consistent habit of being the self you want to represent to the world and do it over and over again. Until it becomes the only way in which you know how to be and act.

The
Practice of
PIVOT

Bringing the entirety of the practices of *PIVOT* into your weekly life, is creating a habit that essentially is a habit of no habit. It is being open to change, being non reactive to it and prepared to take on the unknown. It is taking concepts like *balance* and questioning them and no longer allowing them to be the yardstick used to measure success in your life. Striving to achieve something such as balance (that fundamentally cannot exist in a twenty-four hour day) will be a thing of the past. Or letting go of a tried and tested habit that has to shift the moment the world around you changes. Understand that some actions will be in balance and others will always be out of balance just as easily as some habits will prevail and others will drop off. *Pivot* is not a single action or single result. It is a series of micro-actions resulting in the ability to shift more and change as often and quickly as one needs.

As we pivot we consciously take the time to look at the perspective of our lives and the given situation, using our intuition to check into our core values and our north star. We give ourselves the vision that we want to live into, and this vision can change moment to moment or could be a long journey ahead. It is only then that we can clearly identify any obstacles that may be in our way and determine who needs to be involved and enrolled into the new vision—that is when the clear tactics and next steps to be achieved come to light. The action of pivoting should happen swiftly with ease and all in tandem. Like a song sheet where everyone knows the lyrics and notes without ever glancing down at the piece of paper. The only way to dance with the practices is use it *as* a practice. The rigor you give to your physical workout practice or your marathon training is the same rigor you need to bring to your practice of *Pivot*; with a level of ease and grace un-bestowed to you. When you are inline with the framework there is nothing that can disrupt or break your flow. Using presence, intuition, vision, obstacles, and tactics all in tandem all the time, everywhere and in any situation.

We operate like we are in control, when in fact we are not. We didn't know it before and many of us still haven't realized we are not in control. COVID-19 has forced the hand of everyone on the planet and has pulled us all to look inward. The routine you had with getting your kids to school and yourself to work in the morning, was put to a halt. The comfort of having our children attend a building we call school was no longer, and suddenly the sheer act of getting groceries from the local grocery store became one of the most dangerous acts and placed people at unease. How profound that within one day everything we know to be true about our daily routine was altered. The way you thought you operate your business or career has changed. It all stopped dead in its tracks. Yet, the sun still rose by day and the moon continued to light our paths at night. Mother nature continued her routine. To quote the French expression, "Plus ça change, plus c'est la même chose;" meaning, the more things change, the more they stay the same.

When staying grounded and present, one should be able to anchor into nature and into the natural flow of life, versus becoming consumed by the drastic changes that a global pandemic forced upon the world. Creating routine and consistency is a thing of the past. Adapting and being agile is the now and the future.

If you have made it this far and are still resisting the act of moving and shifting over and over again. I would ask yourself why? Why are you hooked on keeping things the same? What are you resisting? There is a level of comfort that exists in keeping with a routine and having the same mindset. In the past, it was also considered a badge of honor to remain with the same company for a series of years. Decades of service, decades of consistency. Allowing for policy and actions to remain at status quo. You can keep resisting the pivot, the shift, the change, but it is coming for you anyways. The world will no longer put up with old ways of thinking and being. Everything is being confronted and questioned. Things will change. Things need to change. Whether you are ready or not. Because this is a systemic issue, all we know of our society will change. Embrace it, and be the change.

So we provoke and question again, what needs to change in you, so that you can create another version of you? What are you continuing to hold on to that is defining you, but stopping you from receiving any of the material in this book? Perhaps you need to flip back to "Week One: Perspective" and read through again, creating new eyes for yourself. Or perhaps you simply need to make a choice. You see, transformation should happen in an instant. You can spend years searching for it and reading yet another book about it, but everything you need is right there inside the reader holding onto this book, Kindle, smartphone, or listening to the audio. As I shared in the beginning, nothing here is new. The only thing different is the way in which everything is strung together. The only thing new here is that we have never had this conversation on this day in this time. Even if you are giving this a reread. We have never been together at this moment. And listen carefully, this moment—the one right now—it is all you have, it is your only opportunity to act. Who will you be in your life, with your family, and at work if you lived your life this way?

Taking the tools that we have spoken about in this book and using them as practices to anchor yourself, your family, or your teams at work, could support in providing the grounding you need to stay present. The practices of *Pivot* are ones that I continue to use over and over again. When someone is seeking a transformation with their body there are many different routes that they can take. They can choose the fad diet with infrequent exercise where they can generally witness short-term immediate results with some moderate change, or occasionally you will find the individual that has chosen to rip their kitchen cabinets apart and take on their diet by eliminating all refined flour, sugar, and processed foods, and decided that from that moment on they were going to immerse themself in a healthy eating lifestyle. This is generally the same individual who will begin a daily fitness routine that will last years—demonstrating a commitment to the work and making the transition to a complete transformation. Day in and day out. This second method often leads to profound change with lasting results. The long game is the best way to be with the actions of *Pivot*. To get comfortable with pivoting and pivoting often, you must be willing to take on the work. Day in and day out. To pivot is simply not a one-time phenomenon.

Pivoting and change is a practice that is a constant shift and learning cannot be completed in a five-week period. It is a commitment to being open and willing to see a new way. It is a mind shift and a culture that needs to exist within you.

When someone shares with you a statement like, "There's been a change of plans . . ."—what is your initial reaction? What do you think, say, or do? What do you say out loud? How do you respond to that person? Then, what do you say about it to others? Are you even aware of your actions or words? You must be prudent with your actions, what you say, and with your reactions—how you react to every situation you face. But more importantly you must be cautious with your inner dialogue. What are the words you say and don't say to yourself? There is a way of being that has been ingrained deep within you. You likely have no idea of how you react or what you say to yourself or others. If you are mean and judge yourself, you are likely doing the same thing to others. Whether you say it outloud or not. Those words vocalized or not will indeed impact the actions that follow. *"You can't love another, until you love yourself."* (Unknown). Consider that you are self-inflicting paralysis inside of you. You cannot shift or pivot if you are telling yourself, I can't do that or no one would listen to me anyways. Or maybe you are saying who am I to lead a group of people? The negative self-talk we all know is not a constructive way to be. Yet, we all still do it. We are all guilty of consuming it. Why? There is a whole revolt that needs to happen repeatedly within each one of us where we no longer allow negative self-talk. And, if you won't do it for yourself you need to do it for the people around you. They are the ones affected. Don't believe me? Go take a deep look at your kids, their language, their patterns, and their behaviors. For those of you that lead teams, look closer at the way they run meetings, the words they use, and the comments they make. I worked with a respected leader who when asked, "How is your day going?" he would always respond sarcastically with, "Living the dream," which was not what he meant. His sarcasm trickled into the entire organization with one simple phrase and way of thinking. Right there is an example of where a pivot could create a new world of possibility. A pivot doesn't have to be a complete u-turn. In fact it doesn't have to be a turn at all. It is the willingness to question the way things are and wondering if there is anything blocking the way things could be. When faced with a new direction, concept, or opportunity, what would be possible if you were to simply be present with the statement, "There's been a change of plans?" What if you were able to adapt and go with the flow, but still feel in control of your happiness within the new outcome? More importantly, what if you drove the change of plans? Change of direction? Change of conversation? Change in language? What if you were the change agent and not the victim of change?

In my life, I have noticed that I cause a change of plans for myself often—what feels like all the time. At first I thought I was simply bored; needed a new problem and was addicted to drama. Of late, I am realizing that what I am constantly seeking is shift and change. The opportunity to shift the same conversation or complaint. To shift perspective and to shift the narrative. The difference from facing change is that you become the perpetual instigator of change, questioning everything and solving nothing. Once again, I was finding myself in a self-inflicted crisis. However, causing this breakdown in my life allows me the time to question and look at everything. I take the practices of perspective and use them to question what I am seeing and what I am not seeing. What am I doing and what do I really want to be doing? Taking the status quo and demanding more from it. Imagine that—forcing a crisis in your life on purpose. What if we didn't have to wait for the world to shut down to actually re-evaluate everything, even if just in one area of your life?Post-pandemic companies are re-evaluating office spaces, work stations, the number of people in the office, and questioning whether they even need an office at all. Imagine the dismantling of commercial real estate as we know it. If anyone had even brought forth that notion pre-pandemic they would have thought you were crazy. Organizations like Google allowed their offices to be used as homeless shelters while they declared that the workforce will be remote for the remainder of the year. We often get attached to the way things are that we lose the ability to shift perspective and to simply view things another way. What would it look like to question everything, all the time without having judgement of making things wrong or right?

As fear of the pandemic rose, there was a heightened sense of loss and grief that was present in the air, and that feeling is and has been present with many people everytime there is a conversation of change. Our knee jerk reaction is to panic. What if we are able to calm our thoughts and be present? What if we found change exciting?

In the Netflix documentary, *The Last Dance*, when Michael Jordan is asked what made him so successful, his response is his work ethic (of course), but more importantly, his ability to be fully present for whatever was right in front of him, even in the face of change. What would be possible for organizations, individuals, and teams if they were completely present and not worried about a future that hasn't happened yet? It comes back to, what if we lived each moment as though it was our only one? Living a life moment to moment, could provide us with the clarity and freedom to choose the path and pivot freely.

I found it interesting to see the reactions from individuals during a global crisis that was forced upon us; a dear friend of mine said in the thick of the unknown of the COVID-19 pandemic, "You have to appreciate a good crisis." There are so many distinct actions that individuals demonstrate during this sort of time, but you could replace the pandemic with any traumatic life event, devastation, or disappointment. Our actions and non-actions provide insight to what is really going on in our thinking. So to cause a crisis is to force a new way and demand a new perspective for yourself. Do you have the courage to cause a crisis in your own life? To force yourself and demand a new look, especially if everything is "fine"? If there is nothing wrong or nothing that needs to be fixed, do you have the courage to take a deeper look? That is where the real power of pivot lies—in the willingness and ability to force a crisis on yourself and your teams. To demand that there is something different out there for all of you. Especially when you don't want to, or if you don't have enough time, and especially if you are at the height of your game. The fall of empires happened when the leaders were asleep. Relationships crumble when people are taken for granted.

How many times do you say to yourself that there just isn't enough time? *I can't possibly revisit the practices of PIVOT because I just don't have the capacity right now. I don't have the time to invest in what could be, I can't even handle what is happening.* Spoiler alert. There is never going to be enough time. Time is a finite resource of which we all have the same amount of hours in a day to utilize. You will never have enough of it, nor will you even make good enough use of it. You simply need to choose what you do with it.

A "Power Pivot" (perhaps needs to be a concept in a follow up book) is taking a sledge hammer to what you know as your existing life and looking at every piece in a shattered state. It will allow you to see what still fits together and what is a jagged edge that needs to be permanently removed, which then shows you the new space you have to fill. It is forcing us to question and ask why things are done the way they are, over and over again. Day in and day out, in every dark corner of our lives, and at home and at work. It is the act of not stopping when you come up against a difficult situation or question. It is not backing down when people respond with, "It is working fine and you should leave it well enough alone." It is no longer accepting comments like, "If it ain't broke don't fix it." It is taking a stand when you know things will change and evolve, and making the decision to be the match and not the log waiting for the flame to burn you to the ground. What if you acted like no one was coming to save you and it was up to you to be your own hero? The accountability for change does not lay over there with your partner or your colleagues at work. It lies within you. Within each of us.

I believe in the resilience of human beings because there is such a unique opportunity in the world to create and to do so from a place of justice with peace and ease, and to create a place that provides equal opportunity for all. But the only way to do that is to act and not react. In the beginning of the book I made a bold statement. In case you missed it, I will share it again here with you. We are all free to choose, but we are not free from the consequences of our choices. Force yourself to wake up and choose wisely. Change will find you whether you want it to or not. It is coming to a body near you. It's time to make that decision—be the spark and light the match or watch the wood slowly burn. I know my choice, I hope you know yours. Pivot often and wake up every area of your life. Ignite your fire to light the path in whichever one you choose.

Conclusion

As we conclude the practices of *PIVOT*, it is important to remember that it is when actions mirror our words that the miraculous appears. The more we can practice matching what we do with what we say, the more we will get the results that we want.

Take all the thought-provoking questions throughout the book and use them repeatedly to continue to be curious about what would be possible with change. Never stop exploring your options and new roads. What new approach, idea, or relationship is available to you if you are simply willing to pivot?

I remember when I first shared the concept of "change being here" someone said to me, "Can you shift the wording in the subtitle? No one likes change." That is the point. We don't like change, even if we say we do. The thing is, change is inevitable. We are either growing and changing or we are stagnant and dying. It may not be today, it may not be tomorrow, but it is on its way.

If there is one thing that you take from this book, my hope is that you understand pivoting is a phenomenon that is here to stay coupled with change and we must adapt. We must shift our reaction time and train ourselves, our families, and our teammates to react swiftly and concisely. There is no room for our emotional state to interrupt what needs to be accomplished.

No matter what stage of life you are in, it is never too late to begin anew. Let every day be your hour number one. Most importantly, you can do it, you are doing it everyday. The challenge is to do it with ease and grace—over and over again. The more we practice the ebb and flow of change, the easier it will be for you, and for your various teams to dance with you. The melody of change can be something we are all in sync with versus resisting and challenging it.

I hope this book becomes one that you pay forward with and use often.

The concept of *PIVOT* was both inspired and tried by Power Yoga Canada. If you are interested in diving deeper into the concepts of *PIVOT* join us for our Pivot Accountability Coach (PAC) Certification programs (www.pivotmethods.com).

In the end the most important concept is to take yourself on and pivot over and over again, in every and all situations and in every moment. Recreate yourself as often and as quickly as you can.

Change isn't coming, it's here—pivot often.

* * *

Thank you to Kinndli McCollum and Power Yoga Canada (www.poweryogacanada.com) for being my forever playground and the type of business and community that welcomes change head on with open arms—always answering yes.

Pauline Caballero boasts an extensive career in the wellness and yoga field. She is the President and Co-founder of Power Yoga Canada (PYC), a network of hot power yoga studios with the goal of creating a community centered around positive personal transformation. The company has grown to thirteen locations to date, and offers teacher training and certification. She is a Registered Holistic Nutritionist, as well as a certified 500-hour Yoga Alliance E-RYT.

Pauline has also served as a board member with Africa Yoga Project, and is Chief Revenue Officer for Buckland Customs Brokers Ltd.

www.poweryogacanada.com
@poweryogacanada

GOLDEN BRICK ROAD
PUBLISHING HOUSE

Link arms with us as we pave new paths to a better and more expansive world.

Golden Brick Road Publishing House (GBRPH) is a small, independently initiated boutique press created to provide social-innovation entrepreneurs, experts, and leaders a space in which they can develop their writing skills and content to reach existing audiences as well as new readers.

Serving an ambitious catalogue of books by individual authors, GBRPH also boasts a unique co-author program that capitalizes on the concept of "many hands make light work." GBRPH works with our authors as partners. Thanks to the value, originality, and fresh ideas we provide our readers, GBRPH books are now available in bookstores across North America.

We aim to develop content that effects positive social change while empowering and educating our members to help them strengthen themselves and the services they provide to their clients.

Iconoclastic, ambitious, and set to enable social innovation, GBRPH is helping our writers/partners make cultural change one book at a time.

Inquire today at www.goldenbrickroad.pub